Lee Hooper

Empathetic Education: An Examination of the Applicability of Humanistic Theory in New Zealand Classrooms

GRIN Verlag

Bibliografische Information der Deutschen Nationalbibliothek:

Die Deutsche Bibliothek verzeichnet diese Publikation in der Deutschen National-
bibliografie; detaillierte bibliografische Daten sind im Internet über http://dnb.d-
nb.de/ abrufbar.

Dieses Werk sowie alle darin enthaltenen einzelnen Beiträge und Abbildungen
sind urheberrechtlich geschützt. Jede Verwertung, die nicht ausdrücklich vom
Urheberrechtsschutz zugelassen ist, bedarf der vorherigen Zustimmung des Verla-
ges. Das gilt insbesondere für Vervielfältigungen, Bearbeitungen, Übersetzungen,
Mikroverfilmungen, Auswertungen durch Datenbanken und für die Einspeicherung
und Verarbeitung in elektronische Systeme. Alle Rechte, auch die des auszugsweisen
Nachdrucks, der fotomechanischen Wiedergabe (einschließlich Mikrokopie) sowie
der Auswertung durch Datenbanken oder ähnliche Einrichtungen, vorbehalten.

Imprint:

Copyright © 2013 GRIN Verlag GmbH
Druck und Bindung: Books on Demand GmbH, Norderstedt Germany
ISBN: 978-3-656-51241-7

This book at GRIN:

http://www.grin.com/en/e-book/262259/empathetic-education-an-examination-of-
the-applicability-of-humanistic

GRIN - Your knowledge has value

Der GRIN Verlag publiziert seit 1998 wissenschaftliche Arbeiten von Studenten, Hochschullehrern und anderen Akademikern als eBook und gedrucktes Buch. Die Verlagswebsite www.grin.com ist die ideale Plattform zur Veröffentlichung von Hausarbeiten, Abschlussarbeiten, wissenschaftlichen Aufsätzen, Dissertationen und Fachbüchern.

Visit us on the internet:

http://www.grin.com/

http://www.facebook.com/grincom

http://www.twitter.com/grin_com

249.744 – Essay 1 (Question 1)

Empathetic Education: An Examination of the Applicability of Humanistic Theory in New Zealand Classrooms

Approximate length – 2500 words

Submitted on May 16th 2013

Abstract

Effective learning theories are often a debated area in the educational sector. Humanistic theories offer an approach that both embraces and acknowledges the emotional aspects of the individual learning process. This essay argues that the relevance of humanism towards to the school system is significant, particularly when students begin to show signs of emotional behavioural disorders (EBD). Education from a humanistic perspective looks to implement methods to address the underlying causes that motivate students to act in ways that are both unhelpful to themselves and others in their immediate environment. This can be done through a variety of pedagogical strategies, borrowing on the theories of traditional humanists, such as Carl Rogers and Abraham Maslow, to more modern approaches such as Non-Violent Communication. An outline of some of the pertinent theories and techniques in the humanist approach will be given, alongside their applicability in a New Zealand school context with students who show signs of EBD. Incorporating a culturally-aware approach will also be demonstrated to hold significant value, with relevance to those of both Maori and European heritage. It is concluded that empathetic educational practices provide students and teachers with opportunities to grow and learn together in a symbiotic environment.

Introduction to Humanism

Humanism began as a reaction during the 1950s towards the more mechanical and deterministic aspects of behaviourism and psychodynamic theory, with both approaches being criticised as dehumanising (Weiten, 2011). Whist there are many facets of humanism, its general intention is to emphasis the individual and their potential for human growth. Importance is placed on the individual's subjective experience of reality, alongside their ability to consciously choose how reality is perceived and changed (Entwistle, 2012). In addition, while humanism takes some of its theoretical origins from existentialist theory, in regards to the idea that individuals are free and responsible to decide meaning for their own lives, it focuses on the more positive aspects of the theory, such as curiosity, spontaneity, and the disposition towards self-actualising full potential (Wong, 2006). These facets mean that humanism takes an optimistic view towards human nature. In relation to education, humanistic principles focus on the self-directed learning, autonomy, and nurturing self-development and personal growth (Leonard, 2002).

Key theories and concepts

One of the key figures in humanism is Abraham Maslow, who set out the *hierarchy of needs* (Gordon & Browne, 2012). This theory proposes that humans have an intrinsic drive towards personal development. Maslow described this as a "systematic arrangement of needs, according to priority, in which basic needs must be met before less basic needs are aroused" (Weiten, 2011, p. 394). Basic needs include physiological needs, safety and security, esteem needs, belongingness and love needs, through to higher ones, such as cognitive needs, aesthetic needs, and self-actualisation (Braungart & Braungart, 2006). The process towards fulfilling each need before moving onto the next is one of dynamic movement, and in the educational environment, reflects process of individual growth and development.

Another major figure in the humanistic approach is Carl Rogers, whose 'person-centred' theory emphasises self-actualisation through personal growth training (Finger & Asun, 2001). Attention is placed on 'the self', a construct that encompassed a "collection of beliefs about one's own nature, unique qualities, and typical behaviour" (Weiten, 2011, p. 392).

When an individual's perception of self differs too much from actual experience, psychological imbalances occur. In a school context, one way of creating incongruence between self and experience is when the teacher uses positive conditional regard. An example of this is when a student who follows and excels in school protocol is rewarded, such as through praise, social recognition or grades. Rogers (1977) argues that this inhibits personal emotional growth through students being made dependent on the positive affirmation of others. Kohn (1999) elaborates on this further, stating that people lose intrinsic motivation when they are rewarded or punished. This occurs through the reward or punishment taking over as the primary stimulus, which is to be either gained or avoided. As an alternative, Rogers asserts that unconditional regard plays an important role in fostering self-development (Rogers, 1977). Applying this concept to education, unconditional regard towards students will help to bring about congruence between their self-image and the environment around them. This encourages the creation of a caring and empathic school setting that facilitates student growth, particularly for those with EBD, since this approach addresses their primary unmet needs and does not decrease intrinsic motivation.

The influence of humanistic concepts can also be seen in more modern approaches, with non-violent communication (NVC) incorporating concepts from Maslow, Rogers, and Kohn into its own theory (Rosenberg, 2003a). The principles of this approach are centred on interpersonal communication involving empathetically listening and honestly expressing, which both utilise a four step process: observations, feelings, needs, and requests. The first step is to have a clear distinction between observation and evaluation in order to specify the behaviours and conditions that affect the individual. This creates 'clean' observations, separate from judgements. The second step is identifying what feelings are present and being sure to differentiate between feelings and thoughts. This helps to give clarity to the situation. The third step is to find out the underlying needs behind the feelings. This brings awareness to what needs are, or are not, being met. The final step involves requesting in a positive and concrete way, how exactly the needs can be met. Rosenberg states that using an NVC approach brings awareness to what "is alive in others", as well as ourselves (Rosenberg & Eisler, 2003, p. 54). In relation to its use in schools, NVC can increase skills in mediating conflicts, help students to feel more engaged and responsible towards their learning process, and providing a non-judgmental way to interpret and respond to behaviour (Hart & Kindle Hodson, 2003). This last point holds particularly significance in relation to students with EBD, as attaching labels to students with behaviour issues can create 'self-fulfilling prophecies', whereby continual behavioural patterns are reinforced by both the teacher and the student (Kauffman & Landrum, 2013).

Applicability of the Humanistic approach in an educational context

In terms of translating theory into practice, Aloni (2011) outlines six important features in developing a humanistic school culture. These are multifaceted student personalities, social climate, dialogue, community and social involvement, student intellectual powers, and teaching techniques.

Multifaceted student personalities

This concept refers to developing versatile and eclectic tastes, both within the mind and outside onto one's environment (Aloni, 2011). Internally, the student would be encouraged towards a positive self-image with traits such as acceptance, empathy, curiosity, and autonomy, alongside the nurturance of intellectual and emotional intelligence. On an external level, the teacher would help to cultivate both human and nature interests in order for the student to become a more holistic social being. In a recent review of several studies on humanistic school counselling and student performance, it was found that cultivating multiple areas of personality, such as empathy, problem-solving, and flexibility, facilitated learning and growth in school environments (Villares, Lemberger, Brigman, & Webb, 2011)

Social climate

According to Maslow (Weiten, 2011), once the primary and basic psychological and emotional needs of a human being are met, they are then free to strive towards optimal conditions where self-actualisation may be reached. Basic conditions include providing a sense community within the school, where there is a commonality between students and teachers, alongside personal attention and respect (Aloni, 2011). On the contrary, when these necessary conditions are not met, student hostility and aggression, alongside other disciplinary problems associated with EBD, become more prevalent. In acknowledging that the student's environment is a key factor in the learning process, teachers and school counsellors alike are able to provide conditions that ensure a positive social climate (Lemberger, 2010).

Dialogue

By utilising various pedagogical dialogues, a multifaceted approach to interpersonal communication will help students to strive towards higher mental and emotional states of being (Aloni, 2011). For instance, Socratic methods can be used to create critical discourse in a way that allows students to uncover ideas from a method self-discovery. Another approach can be to use NVC in establishing a dialogue based on present feelings and needs. There are a multitude of different and creative ways to establish dialogue between students and teachers. For example, in a case study involving a child with EBD, it was found that using child-centred play therapy as a way to address self-concept issues was effective in helping the child develop more positive and constructive interpersonal relationships in his classroom (Cochran, Cochran, Fuss & Nordling, 2010). The important aspect of applying dialogue in a humanistic sense is that a quality connection is made between the teacher and the student.

Community and social involvement

This revolves around integrating the wider community and generating a symbiotic relationship between the school and those involved in it, both directly and indirectly, as well as social organisations that play a positive role in the community's development (Aloni, 2011). One example of this is to collaborate with parents in helping enhance and shape curricular activities. Another would be to encourage students to participate in student mentoring programs, alongside the option of contributing to creating regulatory processes inside the school. In addition to cultivating these types of relationships, support systems would be also be in place for those students who are "culturally deprived, economically disadvantaged or physically and mentally challenged" (Aloni, 2011, p. 43).

General education program

This constitutes learning the foundational aspects of education and culture so that students can act in "complex, effective, and meaningful ways" (Aloni, 2011, p. 44). This means thinking philosophically about matters, alongside having a healthy scepticism of accepted truths, developing cognitive skills and having metal flexibility, and fostering artistic literacy to cultivate diverse interests and spark creative imagination. These areas would naturally be in addition to learning the sanctioned curriculum, so that integration into the social structure of society after school will be more accessible.

Teaching techniques

These include making sure that what is being taught is in fact congruent with the students' needs and has 'real world' applications, having a varied and comprehensive approach to student assessment that takes into account the different aspects of learning, intelligence, and creativity, and replacing disciplinary-based programs with educational and developmental ones (Aloni, 2011). In terms of applying humanistic concepts to students with EBD, the teacher would need to be aware that multiple cases are likely and that a holistic approach, encompassing numerous interpersonal methods, is required (Chaplain, 2003).

Applying Humanistic concepts to New Zealand schools

Applying humanistic concepts to New Zealand schools can be done on both the macro and micro level. Realistically, the ability of a teacher to incorporate this approach into their daily teaching schedule will depend on the type of school they find themselves in; at a socio-economic level, decile rating, and cultural and geographic position (Church, 2003; Veugelers, 2011). For those teachers fortunate enough to have a school administration that values a humanist approach, practices and general guidelines may already be in place to facilitate the teaching process. An example of this is seen at Unlimited Paenga Tawhiti secondary school in Christchurch, New Zealand (J. Gallagher - teacher at Unlimited, personal communication, May 10, 2013). In this school there is a focus on students becoming independent learners, building teaching programs around individual passions and interests, self-evaluation, and having frequent community contact in the form of field trips. Furthermore, teachers and students interact on a first name basis, with groups of 15 students having a 'homebase' consisting of learning advisors who are there to help and support students academically and psychologically. Teachers in this environment are encouraged to meet the needs of students on multiple levels, as well as to take the time to work with students with EBD in order to uncover whatever difficulties are present.

For the teacher who finds themselves in a school that does not emphasise a strong humanistic approach, there are also ways to incorporate humanistic principles into their own private practice. At the classroom level, teachers can pay attention to ensure that the basic needs of students are met, avoid using punishments and rewards to motivate students, and adopt NVC principles in the way that they communicate (Kohn, 1999; Rosenberg, 2003b; Weiten, 2011). This last approach is particularly useful in creating a classroom language where students feel open and safe to discuss their feelings and needs (Rosenberg & Eisler, 2003). For example, a Danish study found that NVC helped to reduce conflicts and difficult issues in a classroom environment (Pedersen & Rasmussen, 2008). The results of this study indicated the importance of teaching NVC at an early age and how it can be an effective tool in classroom communication. The significance of this research on students with EBD is that it addresses the needs behind the disruptive behaviours. For instance, the reason why a student may be acting loud and aggressive in class may be caused by an underlying need for attention at that moment. By openly asking and offering the student what they need, instead of punishing them, a fundamental change is allowed to occur in their behaviour (Rosenberg, 2003b).

In terms of applying humanistic principles in a culturally relevant way in New Zealand, Forsyth and Kung (2007) recommend drawing on a Maori-based philosophy called take pū of Āta. This approach looks to integrate Maori values and beliefs in a holistic and humanistic way through developing genuine relationships between students and teachers. Self-reflection, empathy, and the space to express oneself are given primary emphasis so that cultural values are acknowledged and respected. In an ethnographic study evaluating the practical benefits of incorporating Āta into teaching a multi-ethnic group, Forsyth (2011) found the approach to decreased feelings of separation between teacher and student, bringing about more open communication and respect for each member's cultural values. The significance of this study is that it highlights the potentiality of culture as a driving force for applying humanistic theories in a New Zealand environment. Furthermore, it can show teachers of European heritage how to "enter, engage in, and exit relationships" with students from other cultures in a humanistic way (Forsyth, 2007, p.5). In addition, because

7

of the high prevalence of EBD in Maori and Pacific Islander children, due to a disproportionate prevalence in lower socio-economic levels, embracing a culturally aware approach merits even more consideration (Church, 2003).

Assessing the strengths and weaknesses

One of the major strengths in applying a humanistic approach in education is that it "focuses on phenomenology of the whole person rather than on unconscious mind and observable behavioural patterns" (Pearce, 2009, p. 479). Students are treated as holistic and dynamic beings, rather than being reduced to a collection of behaviours, ideas or drives. In doing so, humanism emphasises the positive aspects of human nature and looks to promote growth, rather than diagnose and cure. Furthermore, since the approach is person-centred, its methods are closer to 'ordinary' ways of connecting and communicating, which makes interpersonal connection more natural. In relation to EBD in New Zealand schools, humanism in education provides an effective method to manage and address behavioural issues in an emotionally and culturally responsive way (Pronchow & Macfarlane, 2010).

In terms of its limitations, one criticism of applying humanism in education is that the approach has too much focus at the individual level (McIntosh, Gidman, & Mason-Whitehead, 2011). In doing so, it ignores the sociohistorical context of how the environment of an individual shapes their circumstances. For instance, the reasons for power differences that shape education policy and the structuring schools are not addressed at their fundamental core. Another limitation is that some humanistic concepts, such as self actualisation, cannot be empirically validated or measured, which makes it hard for advocates to scientifically 'prove' that their methods and goals are legitimate (Pearce, 2009). In addition to these theoretical limitations, there are also practical ones. Shifting power from the authoritative teacher figure to collaboration with the student may be difficult for teachers who have a traditional educational outlook. Furthermore, some teachers may find the level that is needed to express oneself for humanistic ideals in the classroom as being difficult or uncomfortable, especially when dealing with students who have EBD (Braungart & Braungart, 2006).

In conclusion, through exploring and assessing the value of humanistic education both theoretically and practically, it is argued that humanist concepts contribute significantly to a positive educational environment. By focusing on the growth and development of students and those with EBD, underlying needs are addressed that can help contribute to effective and holistic learning and education. Humanistic concepts can be applied at a multitude of levels to suit the teacher's ability and school environment, such as linguistically, emotionally, and culturally. Whilst acknowledging that the sole application of humanistic principles would not suit all students, it does provide a solid and potentially liberating educational experience to those who are in need of emotional, as well as intellectual, support throughout their school years.

References

Aloni, N. (2011). Humanistic education: From theory to practice. In W. Veugelers (Ed.), *Education and humanism: Linking autonomy and humanity* (pp. 35-46). Rotterdam, The Netherlands: Sense Publishers.

Braungart, M., & Braungart, R. (2006). Applying learning theories to healthcare. In S. Bastable (Ed.), *Essentials of patient education* (pp.37-62). Sudbury, MA : Jones and Bartlett Publishers.

Chaplain, R. (2003). *Teaching without disruption in the primary school: A model for managing pupil behaviour.* New York, NY: RoutledgeFalmer.

Church, J. (2003). The prevalence of children with severe behaviour difficulties. In J. Church, *Church report: The definition, diagnosis and treatment of children and youth with severe behaviour difficulties* (pp. 54-60). Wellington, NZ: Ministry of Education

Cochran, J., Cochran, N., Fuss, A., & Nordling, W. (2010). Outcomes and stages of child-centered play therapy for a child with highly disruptive behavior driven by self-concept issues. *Journal Of Humanistic Counseling, Education And Development, 49*(2), 231-246.

Entwistle, H. (2012). *Child-centred education* (2nd ed.). New York, NY: Routledge.

Finger, M., & Asun, J.M. (2001). *Adult education at the crossroads: Learning our way out.* London, U.K: Zed Books.

Forsyth, H. (2011). *Āta: A theory of best practice in teaching.* Saarbrücken, Germany: Lambert Academic Publishing.

Forsyth, H., & Kung, N. (2007). Āta: A Philosophy for Relational Teaching. *New Zealand Journal Of Educational Studies, 42*(1/2), 5-15.

Gordon, A., & Browne, K. (2012). *Beginning essentials in early childhood education* (2nd ed.). Ipswich, MA: Wadsworth.

Hart, S., & Kindle Hodson, V. (2003). *The compassionate classroom: Relationship-based teaching and learning.* Encinitas, CA: PuddleDancer Press.

Kauffman, J. M., & Landrum, T. J. (2013). *Characteristics of emotional and behavioral disorders of children and youth* (10th ed.). Upper Saddle River, NJ: Pearson Education.

Kohn, A. (1999). *Punished by rewards: The trouble with gold stars, incentive plans, A's, praise, and other bribes.* Boston, MA: Houghton Mifflin.

Leonard, D. (2002). *Learning theories, A to Z.* Westport, Conn: Oryx Press.

Lemberger, M. E. (2010). Advocating student-within-environment: A humanistic theory for school counseling. *Journal Of Humanistic Counseling, Education And Development, 49*(2), 131-146.

McIntosh, A., Gidman, J., & Mason-Whitehead, E. (2011). *Key Concepts in Healthcare Education*. Los Angeles, CA: SAGE.

Pearce, K. (2009). Humanistic perspective. In S. Littlejohn & K. Foss (Eds.), *Encyclopedia of communication theory, Vol 1* (pp. 473-479). Thousand Oaks, CA: SAGE.

Pedersen, A., & Rasmussen, C. (2008). Conflict and communication: learning a new language. *Race Equality Teaching, 26*(2), 44-48.

Pronchow, J.E., & Macfarlane, A.H. (2010). Managing classroom behaviour: Assertiveness and warmth. In C. Rubie-Davis (Ed.), *Educational psychology: Concepts, research, and challenges* (pp. 150-166). London, U.K: Routledge/Taylor and Francis Publishing.

Rogers, C. (1977). The politics of education. *Journal Of Humanistic Education, 1*(1), 6-22.

Rosenberg, M. (2003a). *Nonviolent communication: A language of life*. Encinitas, CA: PuddleDancer Press.

Rosenberg, M. (2003b). *Teaching children compassionately: How students and teachers can succeed with mutual understanding.* Encinitas, CA: PuddleDancer Press.

Rosenberg, M., & Eisler, R. (2003). *Life-enriching education: Nonviolent communication helps schools improve performance, reduce conflict, and enhance relationships*. Encinitas, CA: PuddleDancer Press.

Veugelers, W. (2011). Introduction: Linking autonomy and humanity. In W. Veugelers (Ed.), *Education and humanism: Linking autonomy and humanity* (pp. 1-8). Rotterdam, The Netherlands: Sense Publishers.

Villares, E., Lemberger, M., Brigman, G., & Webb, L. (2011). Student success skills: An evidence-based school counseling program grounded in humanistic theory. *Journal Of Humanistic Counseling, Education And Development, 50*(1), 42-55.

Weiten, W. (2011). *Psychology : themes and variations* (8th ed.). Belmont, CA: Wadsworth/Cengage Learning.

Wong, P.T.P. (2006). Existential and humanistic theories. In J.C. Thomas & D. L. Segal (Eds.), *Comprehensive handbook of personality and psychotherapy: Vol. 1. Personality and everyday functioning* (pp. 192-211). Hoboken, NJ: John Wiley.